Finding
Adventure in the
Ordinary

Finding Adventure in the Ordinary

a survival manual for uninspired parents

Mayo Mathers

MOODY PUBLISHERS
CHICAGO

Scripture quotations marked NKJV are taken from the *New King James Version*. Copyright © 1982 by Thomas Nelson, Inc. Used by permission. All rights reserved.

Scripture quotations marked NIV are taken from the *Holy Bible, New International Version*®. NIV®. Copyright © 1973, 1978, 1984 by International Bible Society. Used by permission of Zondervan Publishing House. All rights reserved.

Scripture quotations marked NASB are taken from the *New American Standard Bible*®. Copyright © 1960, 1962, 1963, 1968, 1971, 1972, 1973, 1975, 1977, 1995 by The Lockman Foundation. Used by permission.

Scripture quotations marked TLB are taken from *The Living Bible*. Copyright © 1971. Used by permission of Tyndale House Publishers, Inc., Wheaton, Illinois 60189. All rights reserved.

Section 1 first appeared in the August 1995 issue of *Living with Teenagers*.

Section 4 (from the beginning to just before "Christmas—Perfect for Preserving Memories") first appeared in the September/October 1994 issue of *Today's Christian Woman*.

Section 7 first appeared in the September/October 1999 issue of *Today's Christian Woman*.

ISBN: 0-8024-1420-6

1 3 5 7 9 10 8 6 4 2

Printed in the United States of America

Dedication

To my mother, Zell Randall, who parented my brother, sister, and me with great pizzazz; and to my father, Howard Mayo, whose untimely death prevented him from raising us into adulthood but who, nevertheless, left an indelible mark of love on our family.

To my husband, Steve, who consistently encourages me as a wife and mother and who always cheers me on in my speaking and writing.

To Nancy Kitchen and Carrie Langford, national representatives with Stonecroft Ministries, who first conceived of the "Creative Parenting" seminars that led to this book and then created the opportunities for me to present them.

And especially to my delightful sons, Tyler and Landon, who love me in spite of my parental fumblings, who submitted fairly cheerfully to my various ideas to improve our family life, and whose quick sense of humor prevents me from taking myself too seriously.

Table of Contents

Disastrous Illusions

My earliest memories are of belonging to a perfect family—pure *Leave It to Beaver* stuff. My father was a schoolteacher and my mother a homemaker. Even as a small child, it was clear to me that my mother loved what she did. Each day, just before Dad came home from school, she changed into a dress, freshened her makeup and hair, and then, while she brewed coffee for him and tea for herself, she allowed me to arrange a pretty serving tray. When Dad walked in the door, there we stood waiting to welcome him home. With such an example as hers, it's no wonder that the only thing I ever wanted to be when I grew up was a homemaker.

What a shock to discover after marrying my husband, Steve, that for me, the reality of homemaking was a deadly redundancy. Every day the same beds had to be made, the same floors swept, the same dishes washed. There was nothing stimulating to me about the process. I decided it must have been parenting my mother found so intriguing.

However, after the birth of our two sons, Tyler and Landon, it was just more of the same. Those two little boys refused to stay clean and fed! Every day I had to do everything all over again—several times a day! It made me irritable, and my family responded in kind.

When I asked my mother what her secret was, she just laughed. "No secret, honey, I just loved your father and I loved you kids."

Well, I loved my family too, but it seemed not to be enough. My lack of parenting aptitude distressed me deeply. *What kind of woman doesn't enjoy caring for her family?*

Then one awful morning, when Tyler was in second grade and Landon in kindergarten, I reached the end of my limits. For the third morning in a row my sons had stomped out of the house in angry tears. Tyler couldn't find the schoolbook he needed, and Landon couldn't find the shirt he wanted to wear. Little stuff—always little stuff—that created major crises.

As the door slammed behind them, I slumped to the floor in my own heap of frustrated tears. *I absolutely could not survive one more day of this existence.* Something had to change—and change fast—before my family left me or I left them. I did not want to lose what mattered most to me. Surely there had to be a way to make family life and homemaking less tedious and stressful. But where on earth could I start?

After calming down, I got out a pen and paper and made a list of all the things I wanted our sons to learn while growing up in our family. When the list was completed, I consolidated it into four main thoughts:

- ☒ I wanted God to be a tangible influence and the prime motivating force in their lives.

- ☒ I wanted them to believe that life is an adventure and far too precious to waste even one minute being bored.

- ☒ I wanted them to understand that what they possess mentally is far more precious than anything they'll ever possess materially.

- ☒ I wanted them to have a strong sense of family heritage and pride and to know that their very best friends were the people they lived with.

Coming up with this list was the easy part! Now I had to figure out how to make it happen. *God, please help me make these ideals a reality,* I prayed, lifting the paper heavenward. *Help me be the mother they deserve.*

With a huge sigh, I got up from the couch and went into the kitchen to begin cleaning up from breakfast. As I put things away, my eyes lit upon a large can of instant hot cocoa, and the first glimmer of an idea came to my mind.

The next morning, thirty minutes earlier than usual, I woke the boys up by serving them two steaming cups of hot cocoa in bed. They were so excited about this unusual occurrence that they didn't even notice that I'd gotten them up earlier than usual. While they sipped their cocoa, I sat on their bed and we discussed our plans for the upcoming day. When they'd finished their drink, I told them I had a surprise, but in order to participate they had to be dressed, have their morning chores done, have their book bags by the door, and be seated at the breakfast table within the hour.

Tyler and Landon would do anything for a treat! In no time at all we were sitting around the table, eating a calm, relaxed breakfast. The treat was nothing more than a flashcard game I had purchased the day before. But by getting them up just a bit earlier than usual, we had time to play for a few minutes. That morning the boys left the house laughing, and I knew we had just turned a crucial corner in our lives together.

The trick now was to keep the momentum going.

I realized that, if I wanted to instill in my sons an attitude of anticipation toward life, I had to set the example. I began to feel like the woman in the eighteenth chapter of Luke who repeatedly went before the unjust judge, pleading for justice. Each day I pleaded with God to inspire me with ideas to relieve the tedium of daily life. I also read everything I could find on parenting and kept my ears open around people who appeared to possess the secret to a successful family life.

Gradually, I began implementing these ideas. Some were such a roaring success that I still use them. Some worked for a while, and others were such complete flops that I discarded them immediately.

The following pages contain these ideas as well as others that I've collected over the years. Just as in our family, some will work for you and some won't. *None* of them will work forever. I quickly learned the key secret to keeping life interesting is to simply stay out of a rut. Don't let your days become predictable.

You know your family best. Take these ideas and modify them to fit you. Use them as stimulus for your own ideas. But don't make the mistake of assuming your family won't enjoy something. Give the idea a try before tossing it out. And above all—*have fun!*

Making God Relevant

There was no area of parenting in which I felt more insecure than that of instilling in my sons a desire to walk with God—and none about which I felt more passionate and desperate. That Tyler and Landon would grow up to be fervent followers of God was a prayer I'd have willingly given my life to see answered. Yet I had no clue how to make it happen. Steve was just as clueless.

It didn't help that everyone offered different advice. Our confusion intensified because one person's advice made perfect sense to us—until someone else offered different advice. Then what *they* said sounded right.

When our sons were in their early teens, there was much debate among our peers about whether or not Christian kids should be allowed to listen to rock music. During this time I attended a seminar in which a well-known speaker sang the praises of Petra, a popular Christian rock group.

"I think it's great that kids have a positive alternative to the world's music," he enthused. "It allows them to worship God in their own language." By the end of the conference, he had me convinced. With

Steve's approval I bought the boys a Petra CD. They were delighted. For weeks, the screech of Christian rock reverberated from their room.

Then I went to another parenting seminar, given by another well-known speaker. "Do *not* cave in to the pressure of Christian rock," he proclaimed vociferously. "You will only develop a taste for the world in your kids." His admonition horrified me. He made sense, but what was I to do? The damage was already done.

I felt like the double-minded man described in the first chapter of James, tossed to and fro by crushing waves of doubt and insecurity.

One morning, after praying about this, I sensed God's gentle rebuke. *I am not the author of confusion,* He whispered. *Your confusion comes from turning to others for advice more than you turn to Me. I know your sons; I know how they are made. Trust Me to guide your parenting. Read My Word when you need advice. You'll find every answer there.*

When I began turning *first* to Scripture for guidance, many of my insecurities were put to rest. God's Word enabled Steve and me to discern what advice lined up with His will and what didn't. God is the only infallible resource for parenting. I knew *He* would not mislead us. Most important, I finally realized that until *I* learned to access God first and foremost, I could not teach my children to do the same.

Parenting is a walk of pure faith. Although a parent may plant the seeds of truth early in his child's heart, it may be many years before they sprout. The important thing is that you, as a parent, never give up on your child's relationship with God. Pray without ceasing for his spiritual solidarity. Train him as God leads you and then, in faith, leave the harvest to God.

Leading Your Child to Christ

When Landon was four years old he began to question me about God and sin and heaven. The depth of his questions startled me. At first my answers were casual, assuming his questions stemmed from things he'd overheard at church rather than from a true spiritual conviction. But his questions intensified, and he seemed genuinely concerned about his soul.

Finally I talked to my pastor about it. "Is it possible for Landon to truly understand his need for God's forgiveness at this age?"

"Absolutely!" he assured me. "Take his questions seriously."

Several nights later, Landon called me back into his room after I'd put him to bed. He was crying.

Kneeling beside his bed, I gathered him in my arms and asked what was wrong.

"I need to ask Jesus to forgive my sins," he sobbed. "Will you pray with me?"

I very simply went through the gospel message, making sure he understood everything I said. Then I asked if he was ready to talk to Jesus.

He nodded his head confidently and slipped out of bed to kneel beside me. His prayer was the sweetest, purest prayer of repentance I have ever heard, and as we knelt there together I knew we were on very sacred ground. The room was saturated with the presence of God.

A year or two later, when Tyler accepted Christ, I overheard the boys discussing it.

"How do you feel now?" Landon asked his brother.

"I have a stomachache!" Tyler exclaimed.

"Oh, that's probably just because when your sins left your heart they dropped into your stomach," Landon assured him.

When your child begins to show an interest in his spiritual condition, discuss the steps to salvation with him, keeping the information simple and clear. Choose a few basic Bible verses to illustrate your words. For example:

1. "The Bible tells us that every single person is a sinner and, because of our sins, we will die" (Romans 3:23; 6:23). Be sure your child understands that sin is simply living selfishly, leaving God out of their life.

2. "However, God loved you so much that He sent His only Son, Jesus, to come to earth and die for you so you can one day live with God in heaven" (John 3:16).

3. "The best part of the whole story is that, when Jesus died for you, He didn't stay dead. Three days after He was buried, God brought Him back to life (Romans 10:9). Right now He's in heaven with God, and He wants to be your very best friend."

4. "Do you believe that Jesus died for your sins? Do you want

Him to forgive you for those sins? Then all you have to do is tell God that."

If he is ready, help your child pray. Again, keep it very clear and simple.

Dear God,

Thank You for sending Your Son, Jesus, to die for my sins. Please forgive me of all my sins. Please come into my heart and help me to live the way You want me to live. Thank You for loving me and letting me live with You forever. In Jesus' name, Amen.

5. **After your child has finished praying, affirm what he has just done: "The Bible says that now you belong to God; you're one of His children (Romans 8:15–17). You will never be alone now because God is your heavenly Father, and He will always be with you wherever you are."**

Family Devotions

Steve and I knew the importance of having family devotions but found it took great determination to get them established in our home. First, there was the challenge of finding a convenient time for the whole family. This changed with the age of the kids. When they were small, bedtime worked well; later we switched to dinnertime and finally settled on breakfast devotions. The point is, find the time that works best for your family but be willing to change as your family's schedule changes. The second challenge was finding appealing material. Just as with all aspects of our life, I found variety to be the secret to successful family devotions. Sometimes we used devotional books, sometimes other tools. Consider these ideas:

☒ **Bible games.**

☒ **Contemporary stories with a moral.**

☒ **Discussion of current moral or ethical issues.** This is a great devotional tool for teenaged children, but give them advance notice so they can mull over their opinions. Show respect for their opinions even if you don't agree. This will keep the discussion open and nonthreatening. Have pertinent Bible verses ready to reference as well as applicable articles.

☒ **A family testimony night where everyone shares what God is doing in their life.**

☒ **Scripture reading using a translation your kids can relate to.**

☒ **Prayer.** Always pray. Be sure every family member participates and be sure to include all aspects of prayer (worship and thanksgiving, forgiveness and cleansing, petition and intercession).

A Tip on Family Prayer

Sentence prayers are a natural, unintimidating means of communicating with God when praying aloud in a group. It takes the pressure off your shyer family members while preventing your "prayer pros" from hogging all the time. It also naturally broadens the scope of your prayers.

Begin by having your family pray short sentences of worship and thanksgiving. For example:

"Lord, You are awesome."
"Thank You for dying for my sins."
"What an incredible world You have created for us."

When the conversation slows down, move on to forgiveness and cleansing:

"Lord, forgive me for being grouchy with my brother yesterday."
"I'm sorry I lied to Dad. Please help me to be truthful."
"I'm sorry I complained about helping Mom."

Continue in this way through all the elements of prayer.

Other Ideas for Making God Relevant

☒ **The God Can.** Label a large, empty can with the words God Can. Put a pencil and pad of paper inside. Every time someone has an answer to prayer, write it down and put the paper in the God Can. Once a month or so during family devotions, open the can and read all the answers to prayer. A reverse idea is to fill the can with dated prayer requests and then pass them out to be prayed for during devotions.

☒ **Prayer Chains.** Cut construction paper into 5" × 1" strips. Each time a prayer is answered (no matter how small) or someone in your family receives a blessing, write it on one of the strips, tape it into a circle, and add it to another strip, forming a chain. Tape the chain on the wall, up near the ceiling, and see how long it takes to surround your dining room with a chain of answered prayers and blessings.

☒ A journal of prayers, answers, and blessings.

◆ **A Gratitude Journal.** Oprah Winfrey encourages her audience to make a daily list of five things they are thankful for. What a great family project! It is of great importance to develop a heart of thankfulness in our children because God places a high value on a spirit of gratitude. Don't allow your children to become oblivious to the simple wonders around them. A spirit of gratitude, more than anything else, will prevent life from becoming tedious.

☒ **Christmas Card Prayers.** My friend Carol and her husband divide up the cards they receive each day during the Christmas season and pray for the people who sent them. I love knowing I'm going to be prayed for on the day they receive my card!

☒ **Prayer and times of Bible reading you and your husband share.** Your kids need to be very familiar with the sight of their parents praying and reading the Bible.

☒ **Teaching your kids to read the Bible for themselves.** Each morning when I took hot chocolate in to the boys, I handed them their Bibles so that they could read a chapter before getting up. Then over breakfast we'd talk about what they'd read.

☒ **Making Sunday your children's favorite day of the week.** This advice came from my Uncle Wayne. "Sundays can be so hectic," he told me when my kids were little. "Getting everyone up, fed, dressed, in the car, and in a 'church-worthy' mood is a huge challenge." He suggested that we create a few "Sunday only" treats to avoid Sunday morning stress. "Let them have sugar-frosted cereal or donuts for breakfast—something out of the ordinary so that they'll look forward to Sunday mornings."

The best way to make God relevant in your children's lives is to make Him a relevant part of every day. Make it a natural thing to stop and pray when discussing problems or concerns. Bring God into your casual conversations. Let Him be your first resource rather than your last. Frequently verbalize your thankfulness—for the weather, your home, a treat, a pleasant evening—every single part of the day.

My mother was great at this. "Good morning, Lord!" she sang out every morning as she pulled open the drapes. "What do You have for us today?"

She maintained this attitude even through the dark days of new widowhood when she found herself alone with three small children and no means of support. She decided to become a teacher so that her work schedule would match our school schedule. But first she had to go to college. The five years between my father's death and her first paycheck were financially lean, to put it mildly.

Although I now realize that she must have had moments of intense worry over how she would make ends meet during this time, my siblings and I were never aware of her concern. She presented everything to us with an attitude of anticipation, an opportunity to see how God would take care of us.

I still vividly recall the summer we went back to Missouri to visit my dad's family.

We had a wonderful time on my grandma's farm, but apparently Mom misjudged how much money the trip would cost.

The day we left for the eighteen-hundred-mile drive back to Oregon, she waited until we were halfway across the state of Kansas to pull the car off to the edge of the road and have a little talk with us.

Turning around to where we sat in the backseat, she said, "Now, kids, God has promised to supply all our needs according to His riches, and God has more riches than you can ever imagine, so you never, ever have to worry."

We stared at her, wide-eyed, wondering exactly what she was getting ready to tell us. I had a feeling that, whatever it was, I *would* worry about it.

"There's only enough money for gas to get the car home," she continued. "There's no money for food or for motels, but we aren't going to worry. We are going to pray."

With that, she bowed her head, asked God to take care of us, and then very calmly started the car back up and headed on down the highway.

A huge silence descended on the car as we kids contemplated the idea of two-and-a-half days without food. *Why, we were starved already! And who wanted to sleep all scrunched up in a car for two nights?*

I slouched down in my seat and shoved my hands into my pockets, contemplating this long trip that now lay ahead of us. When I put my hand in my pocket, I felt a piece of paper. Pulling it out, I found it to be a ten-dollar bill!

"Mom!" I cried in astonishment, holding up the money. "I think God has just supplied our need."

Then I put my hand back in my pocket and pulled out another ten-dollar bill. Now I had everyone's attention, and Mom was pulling back off the road. Five times I put my hand into my pocket and five times I pulled out a ten-dollar bill.

My aunt and uncle had suspected Mom might be short of cash and knew she would never take the money from them. That morning, when they'd hugged me good-bye, they'd slipped the bills into my pocket.

What a celebration we held in the car that day! We fairly danced our way home that summer as we enjoyed the abundance of God's provision in our lives.

There were many other remarkable stories of God's provision dotting my childhood years as Mom taught us to depend on Him for even the smallest need.

Although I was grateful for the comfortable life I now had as an adult, it saddened me to think that Tyler and Landon would never see God in quite the way I had as a child. My unshakable trust in God had been formed as a child when, time and time again, God met the needs of our family. How could Steve and I instill that same level of trust in our sons when we were able to take care of ourselves?

One day, after much prayer about this, it dawned on me that, while I did indeed have many colorful experiences of God's provision in my childhood, they were not what had actually formed my belief in God. My mother was responsible for that. It was her attitude, her faith, her obvious friendship with God that planted the seeds for my own enduring relationship with God.

Our sons would find their own colorful memories of God in the passage of their childhood that would be just as endearing as mine. My responsibility was to see that woven into those memories were the seeds of a sturdy relationship with God, tough enough to weather whatever might be in their future. God would take care of the rest.

Keeping the Correct Perspective

We tend to be shortsighted about life, so caught up in the present that we lose sight of how brief our time on earth actually is. It is easy to attach too much value to the wrong things and assign significance to the wrong accomplishments and, in the process, dilute those things that carry eternal significance.

I learned this lesson when Tyler was in fifth grade. His teacher assigned the class the task of memorizing a portion of the Declaration of Independence, an assignment I took very seriously. I wanted Tyler to get a good grade.

To help him, I typed out the words onto $3'' \times 5''$ cards and taped them to the bathroom mirror and the headboard of his bed. I kept them in the car so that we could practice while driving to and from school. We practiced at breakfast, at dinner, and before bedtime. By the time Tyler had to quote it to his teacher, *any* of us could have gotten an A.

That very next Sunday, as we were driving to church, I opened my Bible to Tyler's weekly memory verse.

"Quick, Tye," I said, "let's learn your Bible verse so that you can get a piece of candy out of the award jar."

The minute the words were out of my mouth, I realized my mistake. I'd just taught Tyler that his teacher's assignment, one that had no eternal value whatsoever, was more important than God's assignment that tells us to hide His Word in our heart that we might not sin against Him.

My mistake wasn't in working so diligently with Tyler on his school assignment. It was in making it more important than the assignment that carried *eternal* value. My actions had made schoolwork vital and God casual.

No matter how successful we are in this life, how wealthy we become, how much we achieve, or how far we go, eternal value is found only in the lives we touch, the people we influence for God. We will take nothing with us to heaven but other people. Fortunately, there's no limit to how many we can take!

Tips for Cultivating an Eternal Perspective

☒ **Pray for specific people your family would like to see become Christians (school friends, neighbors, coworkers).**

♦ *Discuss ways you can "put legs" to your prayers.*

♦ *Invite the people you're praying for to join you for dinner or some other social activity.* I'm extremely shy when it comes to evangelism, but after praying for a man who belonged to the same civic organization I did, we decided to invite him over for dinner. Knowing his interest in foreign travel, we also invited mutual friends who'd recently returned from an African mission trip. Their stories of Africa were a perfect springboard for sharing the gospel. How exciting it was to learn later that the man had begun attending church shortly after our dinner party and had accepted Christ!

♦ *Lend a hand as a family to someone who could use a little help.* Our pastor's family spent an afternoon together doing yard work for a recently widowed young mother.

☒ **Be an anonymous "angel."** Discuss ways your family can anonymously bless someone you're praying for. This kind of "family secret" is a powerful tool for building family solidarity. Our friends, the Routsons, wanted to bless a family that was taking a rare vacation together and used our family as the conduit to give them tickets for a jet-boat trip. How fun it was for us to get to see the family's surprise and pleasure and then pass it back to the Routsons. Three families were blessed by that anonymous act!

☒ **Ask God to give you opportunities to talk to the person you're praying for.** I had been praying off and on for my next-door neighbor ever since her family moved to our neighborhood, but I'd not yet taken the time to get acquainted. "Please make an opportunity for me to visit with her," I prayed one day. That very week I got a letter from a woman in California who had contacted me to speak at a women's retreat she was organizing. She'd just received my promotional package and sent me a very excited note. "Unless they number streets differently in Oregon than they do in California," she wrote, "you must live next door to my dearest friend in the whole world!" It was just the open door I'd needed to call my neighbor.

☒ **Share progress reports with your family.** This keeps everyone excited and encourages them to press on in their own evangelistic goals.

☒ **Celebrate victory!** When I was growing up, any time someone gave his life to Christ at church Mom treated us to an ice cream cone on the way home. You can be sure I was praying rather than fidgeting during the altar calls!

Friendship Evangelism

"Do you think it's wise to let Landon play with Rick?"

Karen's question surprised me as we sipped coffee from a thermos while waiting in her car for our kids' football practice to end. Rick lived in our neighborhood, and he and my son Landon were friends.

"What do you mean?"

"Well, if it were I, I'm not sure I'd let my kids spend time with him. He has such a rough family—I just don't think he's a good influence for Landon."

Later that night I repeated the discussion to Steve, asking his opinion regarding Rick and Landon. We approached the subject from all different angles but kept coming to the same conclusion. *Why expect Rick to be a bad influence on Landon? Why not expect Landon to be a good influence on Rick?*

Philippians 2:15–16 instructs us to be "children of God without fault in a crooked and depraved generation, in which you shine like stars in the universe as you hold out the word of life" (NIV).

It seemed to us that the best way to teach this to our children was not by protecting them from the world but by overseeing them carefully as they walked through it.

We had always limited the amount of time Landon spent at Rick's house while making sure Rick felt welcome in our home. We also took Rick to church with us and stressed the importance of Landon's setting a good example for him and his other friends.

This had been relatively easy until Landon began middle school and it became more difficult to oversee all his activities. We decided it was time to remind Landon of his greatest responsibility to Rick.

"You are the only Christian Rick knows," we said. "It's important that you tell him about Christ. Make sure your actions show him the difference Christ makes in your life."

Together, as a family, we began asking God to give Landon opportunities to witness to Rick. Since Rick went to Sunday school with us, Landon decided to use their Sunday school lessons as a springboard for his witnessing. Before long Rick was ready to ask Jesus into his heart.

The transformation was exciting to watch. Rick became an explorer in an uncharted world. His curiosity was insatiable. Every day after school, before he and Landon headed out to play, they read the Bible. At dinner, Landon repeated Rick's questions about what they'd read, wanting to make sure he was giving him correct answers.

As Rick and Landon continued reading the Bible together, a burden began to build within Rick's heart. He didn't want to ride to church with us anymore. He wanted his parents to go with him. Although Rick and Landon began praying diligently for this, his parents remained uninterested.

Then during the summer, an evangelistic group came to town with a show designed to introduce people to Christ by performing great feats of physical strength. At the conclusion of the show, people struggling with overpowering problems were invited to go forward for prayer. Rick's heart was heavy. He glanced at Landon, and immediately the two of them headed toward the stage. From my seat in the balcony, I watched them go and added a silent prayer to theirs.

Two days later Rick called to tell us not to pick him up for church that morning. "Why?" I asked, my heart pounding in anticipation of his answer.

"My mom's taking me," he said, as if I'd asked a silly question. And I had. *Of course* his mother was taking him.

On our way to church that morning, I thought back over Karen's admonition. Yes, there had been risk involved in letting Landon pursue his friendship with Rick. But watching Rick and his mom pull into the parking lot, I couldn't help thinking of Christ, who risked His magnificent inheritance to share it with me.

There always has been, there always will be risk involved when we follow Christ. But what a reward awaits! I got a glimpse of it in the glow on Rick's face as he held the church door open for his mom.

Making Mealtimes Memorable

Setting the Scene

One piece of advice cropped up repeatedly in all the parenting books I read: Establish a family mealtime around a table. As a result, I decided this was the most logical area to begin improving the atmosphere around our home. The only hitch? I hated cooking. It consumed too much time and made too big of a mess.

Sidestepping the cooking issue, I banked on the old adage "First impressions are lasting impressions" and focused instead on setting the table. My logic was that, if my family sat down to a really great looking table, they would assume the meal would be great as well.

I picked up interesting place mats and dishes at garage sales and secondhand stores and found a booklet on napkin folding. It never took more than five minutes to set a spectacular table and, to my delight, my family took the bait. Seeing the festive table, they sat down expecting a good time—and that's exactly what their expectations created. In no time at all, mealtimes became our favorite part of the day.

It was invigorating to see that a minimum amount of effort had brought maximum results. I began to feel more like my mother and less like a failure. My daily prayer was that God would help me maintain my momentum.

Adding the "Un" to Unusual Table Decor

Let your mind break away from the "norm" in table settings. Look around your house for what you already have on hand that could be used in table settings and go for it. Try these ideas:

- ☒ **Colorful hand towels for place mats and matching washcloths for napkins.**

- ☒ **Magazines or newspapers displaying interesting articles, ads, and headlines.** Discuss the topics while eating.

I once found an ad in our paper that led to a great discussion about how society views a woman's role as wife and mother. The ad announced two upcoming pageants. "Are you the next Miss Central Oregon?" it queried. "Looking for talented young women to compete in our upcoming pageant . . ."

Right beside that announcement was another about the Mrs. Central Oregon pag-

eant. It read "Looking for women to compete for the Mrs. Central Oregon title—NO TALENT REQUIRED." (As if homemaking doesn't require talent.)

☒ **T-shirts and handkerchiefs.** Place the handkerchief and cutlery in the T-shirt pocket and let the lower half of the shirt hang over the edge of the table. (This is a great way to hand out new T-shirts when they're needed.)

☒ **Road maps unfolded to place-mat size.**

☒ **Enlarged (to 11" x 14" size), laminated color copies of vacation photos.** As you eat, reminisce about the vacation. You can also do the same with your kids' artwork or schoolwork. (These place mats make awesome, inexpensive gifts for friends and relatives!)

☒ **Autographed tablecloths.** Your kids will love this because writing on the table is normally a "no-no." Buy a plain white tablecloth (flat bed sheets make great, inexpensive tablecloths) and a box of fabric pens. Have each person at the table sign his name, draw a picture, or write a word of wisdom—whatever strikes his fancy. This makes a wonderful birthday, anniversary, or other special celebration gift when you present the tablecloth to the guest of honor.

Someday I'm going to put a blank tablecloth on my table and leave it there for a few weeks. Whoever comes to our house during that time—be it friend, salesman, or stranger—I'll ask him to sign it and write down his favorite piece of advice. What great dinner conversation it will make as we read the various inscriptions from visitors to our home!

⊠ **Unusual dinner plate combinations.** One of my all-time favorite hints for table settings came from my friend Donna, one of those natural-born homemakers. She sets clear dinner plates over designer paper plates. This transforms one set of dishes into a thousand different designs—just by changing the paper plates beneath them. Talk about cheap! You only need one set of dishes in your cupboard. And, since the paper plates don't get dirty, you can reuse them.

⊠ **Family involvement.** Let each child and even your spouse be responsible for creating the table setting on occasion.

Centerpieces with a Purpose

Choose centerpieces that will stimulate discussion or provide entertainment. For instance:

☒ **World globe.** During dinner, take turns twirling the globe and discussing where you'd most like to travel or live and why. Or twirl the globe and, whatever country your finger lands on, read about it in the encyclopedia. (This would be a great centerpiece to use with roadmap place mats.)

☒ **Games.** Monopoly was our favorite dinner game. We set a time limit, and whoever had the most money and property when the time was up won. I must admit that the game board and money got a bit greasy after a while. Although this didn't interfere with our pleasure, I thought I should warn those of you who are picky about the condition of your games. If you can't stand the thought of grease spots on your play money, consider plastic dominoes. They're indestructible!

My all-time favorite table game is flashcards of any kind. Math, spelling, Bible, you name it, we had flashcards for it. Thanks to flashcards, our kids knew the capitals to every state before they finished first grade! I've found flashcards to be the easiest and least threatening way to learn.

☒ **Several framed photos from family vacations or other special family events.** Spend the mealtime reminiscing about the photos.

☒ **A stack of encyclopedias.** Before or after eating, hand an encyclopedia volume to everyone and see who can find the most interesting fun fact to share.

One night Tyler read to us about a flood that occurred in Boston in 1919. A molasses factory exploded and flooded the city with two feet of gooey molasses. Kids will never find education boring when they're discovering such interesting facts!

☒ **A dictionary.** Take turns picking a new word and see how often it can be worked into the table conversation.

☒ **A stack of videos.** After dinner and cleanup, everyone chooses which one to watch.

☒ **A favorite book.** Kids love to be read to, and around the dinner table is a great place for stories. I chose inspirational and/or educational stories that only took five or ten minutes to read. If longer stories were involved, I continued them from one mealtime to the next.

One of my favorite resources for educational and inspirational stories is Reader's Digest. *They once ran a series of articles entitled "I Am Joe's Body," each featuring a different organ or body part. (This is in book form and available at most public libraries.) I bought a life-sized felt body with removable organs at an educational store and hung it on the dining room wall. Each time I read another "Joe" article, we added the organ to its appropriate location on the body. We learned all kinds of interesting facts during our dinnertime biology lessons. For instance, we discovered that ice cream should never be eaten immediately after a meal because it freezes the stomach and delays digestion!*

Sometimes the centerpiece would be the Bible or a book of poems. Then we'd memorize a poem together or a passage of Scripture. We'd learn one stanza or verse a night until we had the whole selection memorized.

This was one of my favorite mealtime activities but it wasn't Steve's. He was a good sport about it, however, and the boys loved his version of Robert Frost's "Stopping by Woods on a Snowy Evening."

⊠ **Christmas cards.** During the Christmas holidays, open the cards you receive and take turns reading them aloud during dinner. This is a great way for kids to feel connected to distant friends and relatives.

The centerpiece doesn't always have to tie in with an activity. Just look around your house for something interesting. For instance, set a rustic table using a lantern for the centerpiece, your camping dishes for plates, pint jars for glasses, and dishcloths for napkins. Then eat by lantern light.

Beyond the Frivolous

As I mentioned earlier, cooking was not my forte. It took too long and made too big of a mess. However, since it was an inescapable task, I reluctantly admitted that it would behoove me to find a way to relieve the tedious redundancy of meal preparation.

My basic hindrance to enjoying this task lay mainly in the fact that my cooking was in a rut. I shopped the same aisles at the grocery store, bought the same foods, and looked through the same cookbooks.

I decided to venture into new territories and began browsing the more exotic aisles of my favorite supermarket, looking for foods I'd never purchased before. I visited smaller, out-of-the-ordinary food stores that offered selections far beyond the standard fare I was used to buying. I found breadfruit from the islands of the Pacific and cherimoyas from South America. I served blue cornbread made from Mexican cornmeal of the same color and pasta in every shape and color imaginable. None of this added significant time to my day, yet it made meal planning and preparation far more interesting.

Later, when speaking engagements began taking me around the country, I brought home food indigenous to the area I visited. Once I returned from a trip to a coastal city with a box of seaweed soup! It was one of the few times my family put their collective foot down and refused to eat the soup if I prepared it.

"Save it for an example in one of your parenting workshops," they recommended and quickly exited the kitchen.

When on vacation, instead of lugging home silly, dust-collecting souvenirs, we brought home rum cake from the Caribbean, beignet mix from New Orleans, and tea of coca from Bolivia. After we'd been home for a while, we'd bring out the packaged food and relive the experiences of our trip as we looked over our photos.

Add Anticipation to Ordinary Meals (and days)

One morning I told the boys I was fixing a dessert so delicious that they would even eat the bowls when they were finished. They laughed at my wild statement, but as they left for school I heard them wondering together about what dessert I could possibly have planned.

When they walked in the door that afternoon, they immediately started sniffing around.

"So what's for dessert tonight, Mom?" they asked eagerly.

I smiled in satisfaction, knowing my plan had succeeded. They'd obviously spent time looking forward to coming home!

"You'll just have to wait and see," I laughed, "but I guarantee you'll love it so much you'll eat your bowls."

The dessert was just vanilla pudding and fresh fruit, but I had found little bowls made out of chocolate to serve it in. It was the hit of the month, and though I've never served anything in chocolate bowls again, they still remember the night when Mom's cooking was so stupendous that we ate our dishes!

Stay Out of a Rut

This can be accomplished as easily as serving breakfast for dinner or dinner for breakfast. In fact, I once read that the very best breakfast food is pizza! The combination of protein and carbohydrates stimulates the brain and gets it working at maximum power faster than the average breakfast fare. This little bit of news delighted my kids, and pizza became our favorite breakfast!

Another breakfast favorite was "Surprise Muffins." It was just my regular bran muffin recipe, but I folded a couple of dollar bills into tiny squares, wrapped them tightly in foil and dropped them into the muffin cups before baking. We never had leftovers on Surprise Muffin day! Everyone wanted to make sure all the surprises were claimed.

Other Tips for Avoiding Mealtime Ruts

☒ **Make menus.** When the half hour before dinner comes and nothing's defrosted and everyone's tired and hungry, you'll invariably turn to your old standbys.

Making up a menu for the week (or even the month) will not only keep you out of a rut but will relieve you of last-minute "What's for dinner?" stress.

However, don't be the lone ranger in this chore. Involve the whole family in menu planning. Pile cookbooks in the center of the table one night and let the table activity be menu planning. In fact, take this a step further. On the night one child's (or your spouse's) menu choice is being served, let that child help prepare it.

An added benefit to menu planning is that it is a tremendous time and money saver. Grocery shopping is simplified to a very specific list, so shopping is completed much faster, and there are no mad dashes back to the store for missing ingredients. It also cuts way down on pizza deliveries and last-minute passes through fast-food drive-ins.

The most exciting benefit of menu planning was the discovery that, when I knew ahead of time what I was preparing and had all the ingredients on hand, cooking became much less of a chore. I actually began to enjoy meal preparation. And I loved seeing my family have so much fun around the table that they often lingered there for an hour or more.

⊠ **Make extra meals when you cook and freeze them for later use.** If you really get into this, which I did for a time, you can actually cook thirty days' worth of meals in one day and freeze them. This was a lifesaver when the boys were playing sports. I could grab a casserole out of the freezer and put it in the oven while we were at a game, and it would be done when we got home.

The process is simple. Choose ten entrees, make triple of each, and freeze! I discovered that almost everything freezes—just be sure to wrap the dish well with heavy foil to ensure fresh-tasting meals.

☒ **Make grocery shopping an occasional family affair.** This is a great educational exercise to teach your family about budgeting, but it can also be an adventure. Set a monetary limit of three or four dollars and send everyone in search of a never-before-tried food item that can be worked into a meal during the upcoming month.

Take Advantage of the Holidays and Seasons

☒ **Green food for St. Patrick's Day.** Scrambled eggs, biscuits, butter, oatmeal, potato soup, cream sauce, cake, pudding—there's no end to what can be dyed. Add to the mood by having clover-shaped green sunglasses or green plastic derbies on hand for everyone to wear (available at most variety stores).

☒ **Heart-shaped food for Valentine's Day.** My friend of the clear-dishes-and-paper-plates idea cuts her chicken breasts into heart shapes with a cookie cutter!

☒ **Soup served in a hollowed-out pumpkin for a Halloween treat.**

☒ **Individual fruit salads served in cantaloupe halves for a summertime treat.**

Don't Limit the Celebration to Food

☒ During the month of **November,** tape a piece of paper to the refrigerator and have everyone record something they're thankful for before sitting down to eat.

☒ During the month of **July,** keep a list going of the different reasons why everyone's thankful to be an American.

53

⊠ Put party poppers at each plate for a **4th of July** favor.

⊠ For **Easter** put a plastic egg at each place with a slip of paper inside that has a question for that person to answer. (Be sure the questions can't be answered with just a yes or no.) For example:

What historical person would you most like to meet?

What is your favorite Easter memory?

Where would you most like to travel and why?

If you could have any job in the world, what would it be and why?

⊠ Decorate **Christmas** cookies or small **Valentine's Day** cakes to deliver to friends and neighbors.

⊠ Revive the old **May Day** tradition of taking May Baskets to special people. Sneak up to the door, set down the basket, ring the bell, and run away.

One May Day the boys picked tulips from our garden and took them to our next-door neighbor. Unbeknownst to us, she had been battling depression, and the gift of tulips from two little boys was just the medicine she needed. Fifteen years later she still talks about the day Tyler and Landon brought her flowers.

☒ **Go Christmas shopping together for small items you can gift wrap and deliver to nursing homes.** A call to the home will let you know what the residents would find useful.

☒ **Don't limit yourself to the usual holidays.** There are many books that give you a reason to celebrate every day of the year. For instance, did you know August 29 is Edmund Hoyle's birthday? He was an Englishman born at about 1672 who taught people how to play games correctly, which is where we get the saying, "According to Hoyle."

After School Snacks

After School Snack Time was the one event of our day I saw as inviolate. I found no better opportunity for real communication with Tyler and Landon than when they first got home from school and were brimming over with the events of their day. I knew immediately what kind of day they'd had, and my interested presence combined with a simple snack promoted easy conversation. I discovered their communication was more forthcoming when I made a snack for me as well. Perhaps it signaled to them my undivided, unhurried attention; I'm not sure, but once I realized this, I always had three snack plates waiting.

Some afternoons we chatted for barely ten minutes while they bolted down the snack before heading off to other interests; other times they lingered leisurely before finally wandering off, but every minute added to the mortar that held our relationship together.

Visit your local bookstore or library for books on fun, easy, and healthful snacks for kids.

Cheering Up Chores

Working Together "On Time"

After I had a grip on mealtimes, I looked to other areas of family life that would benefit from a little levity. The only thing I found more laborious than cooking was cleaning, so I turned my attention there. The boys had a certain number of daily chores—making their beds, vacuuming, washing dishes—but none of them involved serious housecleaning. I assumed that responsibility myself. Then, when I felt like my hard work was being ignored by their inconsiderate sloppiness, I got cranky. This, in turn, made them cranky—which made for a lot of crankiness around our house.

It finally occurred to me that, if all the cleaning became a family activity, it might alleviate some of the ill will—at least on my part! It would also teach the boys about all aspects of cleaning.

The results were nearly as dramatic as my mealtime endeavors. As soon as the boys had a vested interest in keeping the house clean, they became much more tidy in their habits. To my huge (but private) delight, they also took over the task of nagging Steve to be tidier—and he was much more responsive to their nagging than mine!

My initial inspiration came one Saturday morning when I awoke with the dreaded chore of window washing hanging over my head. I grudgingly gathered a bottle of window cleaner and a roll of paper towels and headed for the family room. There sat our two able-bodied sons reclining lazily on the couch, staring vacantly at Saturday morning cartoons. My irritation begat instant inspiration.

"Hey guys! How'd you like a large Blizzard from the Dairy Queen?" (*Small* Blizzards were a rare treat for us—large ones were unheard of!)

"Yeah!" they shouted in enthusiastic unison.

"OK, then," I said, exceeding their enthusiasm. "It's ten o'clock right now. If we can get the windows washed in one hour, I'll treat you to a large Blizzard of your choice!"

Before they could even groan, I had tossed one of them the cleaner and the other the paper towels. Continuing in an enthusiastic voice, I gave instructions and put them to work. Steve had the bad fortune of walking in on this process. Before he could disappear, I had paper towels in his hands too. As we all worked together, I kept up a running prattle of how good those Blizzards were going to taste. In less than an hour, all our windows were sparkling, and we were down at the Dairy Queen placing our orders.

That morning taught me a very important lesson. Tedious jobs are far less tedious if they have a time limit. Any task can be endured when it's assigned an ending point. Had I just summarily announced, "Boys! Today we wash windows!" I would have had two very resentful kids on my hands as they envisioned their entire Saturday disappearing in a bucket of suds. And in that mood it probably *would* have taken the entire day, not to mention the dubious quality of work they would have produced.

Setting time limits became my most successful strategy for eliciting willing help from my guys. It works really well on Steve, too, when it comes to cleaning the garage.

"Honey," I say sweetly, "how 'bout if you and I spend an hour in the garage tonight?" When he agrees, we set the timer, work until it goes off, and then quit immediately. The next night we do the same, and before we know it, the garage is restored to order—at least for a few days.

More Help-With-Cleaning Tips

☒ **Have races.** True, you do have to monitor this idea and set some parameters to assure quality workmanship, but it works great. Assign each person a room to clean and see who finishes first. No reward needed other than the pleasure of finishing first. Or race to finish a cleaning project before the dinner casserole is through cooking or before the pizza delivery truck arrives. Races of any kind are a great source of energy and enthusiasm. Find the ones that work for your family.

☒ **Hide coins or coupons under lamps or other items that will only be found when dusting under—not around—objects on tables and shelves.** I got this idea after my Auntie Jess came to visit. Several days after she left I found a ten-dollar bill she'd hidden under the plates in the kitchen cabinet. I'd mentioned that I planned to lay new shelf paper that week, and she left me the little treat to find in the midst of my labor.

☒ **Tape a dollar bill around the toilet paper dispenser roll to reward the person who takes time to change rolls.** (This is one of the ideas that didn't work in our family. I was the only one to ever find the dollar.)

☒ **Make chore charts.** Most people enjoy the sense of accomplishment that comes from checking off completed items on a list—especially children. If your child is exceptionally hard to motivate (we had one of those), add the incentive of a reward for a weekly chart that is missing no checks.

☒ **Work to music!** Choose a mutually enjoyable and lively CD, turn up the volume, and watch everyone scurry!

☒ **Plan an activity to follow a big work project so that your family can enjoy the results of their labor.** For example, after a day of yard work, reward your family with a barbecue so that you can relax and enjoy your beautiful yard.

Creative Rewards

We didn't give our sons an allowance. It's not that we didn't believe in it; we just weren't very good with follow-through. Either we'd forget to pay them or didn't have the money on the day it was due. Basically, we just found rewards to be more interesting and far more versatile.

☒ **Coupons.** Computers make these a cinch! Print up a variety of enticements such as, "This coupon entitles the bearer to:

> THIS COUPON ENTITLES THE BEARER TO:
>
> ❏ stay up 15 minutes past bedtime
> ❏ 30 extra minutes of TV
> ❏ skip one chore of your choosing
> ❏ one extra bedtime story
> ❏ 15 minutes of undivided attention
> ❏ one video rental

(Tailor the coupon to your kids' ages and tastes.)

☒ **Post-it Notes.** It is amazing the power of a reward as simple as a note of recognition. When Tyler or Landon did something without being asked or did a kind deed or anything noteworthy, I wrote them a few words of appreciation and stuck it to the headboard of their bed. They loved finding my notes and, to my surprise, saved them. I understood why when I went to bed one night and found a note stuck to *my* headboard:

Dear Mommy, You're the best mommy in the world. I love you.

It was one of the best rewards I've ever received and, just like them, I saved it. Those words spurred me on to be a better parent—which is the whole point of a reward: incentive to be better.

A Word About Rewards

"I think it sets a bad precedent to reward a child for something he should be doing anyway," a woman once challenged me at a workshop I was conducting. "They need to learn real life is not about rewards."

I wholeheartedly *disagree*. Real life *is* about rewards. Who would get up and go to work every morning if they weren't going to be rewarded with a paycheck at the end of the month? What prompts an employee to do his very best—or more than is required on the job—except for the enticement of a raise or better benefits or a commendation from his boss or colleagues?

I'm convinced the reason that full-time homemakers often have a low estimate of their value is directly related to the fact theirs is the one career that doesn't receive a tangible reward for services rendered. They collect no paycheck. There is no promotion to be achieved, no better benefits to be earned for loyalty or longevity of service. Unless a full-time homemaker has a highly appreciative family, it is easy for her to feel undervalued.

Actually, God is the originator of the reward system. Consider the rewards He showers on us for our obedience during our earthly life. Consider the ultimate reward of heaven that He offers to all who believe that Jesus is the Son of God and that He died for our sins. I absolutely believe in, long for, and work toward whatever is available to me from God's hand because I *love* His rewards!

However, the *philosophy* of rewards can be carried to extremes. Not every behavior or action justifies a reward. Some responsibilities should be carried out simply because they must be done in order to maintain a healthy standard of life. We never rewarded the boys for doing their regular, daily chores that were necessary to operate our home at a healthy level of cleanliness. Neither did we reward them for doing something that came with its own built-in reward, such as a cavity-free checkup from the dentist as a result of brushing their teeth regularly and well.

The *definition* of rewards can also be carried to extremes. A reward does not have to be, and often should not be, material. To hand a child a five-dollar bill when a big hug and glowing praise would suffice can result in the development of serious character flaws, such as greed and laziness. It can also alter a child's self-motivation.

Inappropriate or discriminating rewards can pit siblings against each other, and this is deadly to family relationships. When Tyler began kindergarten, his grandmother promised to give him a dollar for every A he received on his report card. Landon was green-eyed with envy when he watched Grandma hand Tyler seven dollars for his first report card. He couldn't wait until he was old enough to go to school and earn money for his grades.

Two-and-a-half years later, Landon finally got to present Grandma with his long-awaited first report card. What none of us had anticipated was the type of report card Landon's teacher issued. She graded her students on everything from tying shoes to cheerful attitudes. As a result, Landon's report card boasted fifty A's!

Now to hand a five-year-old child fifty dollars for his grades is ridiculous. However, to not keep your word to a five-year-old child is devastating. We learned from that experience to be careful with the kind of rewards we promised. After that, Grandma's reward for good grades came in the form of getting to spend the night with her or going out for ice cream.

The best rewards are almost always nonmaterial. Think of rewards that will enhance your relationship with your child. Kids will always be delighted when their reward involves your time and attention rather than your money.

Building Pride, Preserving Memories

Preserving Memories

With the changing face of the family, a sense of heritage and belonging can elude children. Within one family unit might be stepsiblings, half siblings, various parental figures, and a confusing amount of grandparents. Nevertheless, it is vital to a child's emotional well-being that they feel connected to a family group. They also need to be aware of their family's history and feel pride in their heritage.

Suggestions for Building a Sense of Family Pride and Heritage

☒ **Establish family traditions.** Nothing works to instill pride like traditions unique to your family. These don't have to be elaborate or expensive; just something you do together.

When my widowed mother remarried after we kids were grown, her new husband's family had the tradition of having popcorn and 7Up for Sunday night dinner. My kids loved visiting Grandma on Sunday night so that they could participate in the tradition.

One of our family's traditions is to go to a late movie on Christmas night. As the only female in our family, I have to lobby long and hard to keep my guys from choosing something exploding with testosterone, but this simple tradition is something we all look forward to. For the last several years we've been collecting an entourage of people who want to join us in this tradition. Our feeling: "The more, the merrier!"

⊠ **Hold family story nights where everyone takes turns telling favorite family stories.** This is a great way for parents and grandparents to pass on the family's heritage as they share stories from their childhood. The farther back in the family tree you go, the better!

One of our favorite family stories comes from my mom's side of the family. She had six siblings, so obviously there were always disagreements cropping up. One day my grandfather told my uncle to saddle the horse for my aunt, who needed to go to town. Uncle Chuck, however, thought Aunt Martha should be able to saddle her own horse. He knew better than to ignore his father's order, but he decided to use a little latitude in following it. When Aunt Martha went down to the barn to get her horse, it was not the horse she found saddled and waiting but the old milk cow!

Such stories add dimension to the personalities of relatives whom your children have only known as elderly and maybe not too interesting.

☒ **On birthdays, display all the school pictures, photos, artwork, and other mementos of the person being celebrated so that you can reminisce about their life thus far.**

☒ **When on vacation, buy souvenirs that can be used back home to preserve the memories of that trip.** For example, I bought some crazy, colorful fish napkin rings on our Florida vacation. Not only do they make a very festive table, but every time they're used they also remind us of the great trip we had.

  ◆ A fun variation of this idea was mentioned earlier in the book. Have 11″ × 14″ color copies made of your favorite vacation photos and laminate them for place mats. This is cheap and easy and can be done at any office supply or photocopy store.

☒ **Have a Family Photo Night.** Most of us take lots of photos but then put them away and rarely look at them. Whether your photos are carefully organized and beautifully chronicled in photo albums or are stuffed into a box doesn't matter. What matters is that you're enjoying them.

On Family Photo Night it's best to gather around a table, because someone is always going to be saying, "Oh, look at this!" and that's easier done when sitting around a table rather than spread around a room.

I guarantee this will soon become one of your family's favorite pastimes! It's a great way to build a sense of pride and heritage because, as you laugh together over memories and experiences unique to your family, you'll all become convinced that your family is absolutely the best.

⊠ **Have a "Year in Review Night."** The week between Christmas and New Year's is a great time to schedule this activity. Pile the dining table high with journals, photos, and food and dive in for an evening of sheer pleasure.

⊠ **Keep a family journal.** I can already hear the groans from all the committed non-journalers, but please give me a chance to persuade you. Journaling, especially as a family, can be a delightful experience and will give you surprising insight into your children's and spouse's heart as they participate. We tend to be much more self-revealing in our writing than we are in speaking.

Keep the journaling casual and voluntary but always have a notebook handy so everyone can jot down memorable events from their day when the mood strikes. Some variations to journaling you might consider are:

♦ Set aside one night a week (or month) to write in your journal as a family. (Use the journal as a centerpiece at dinner.) Gather input from everyone.

♦ Buy a calendar with large squares on its pages and jot down noteworthy occurrences in the squares. This was the way our neighbors, the Barretts, journaled. All the visitors to their home loved reading their penciled comments and often added comments of their own.

Encourage all family members to participate in the journaling, no matter how young or old. Even invite guests to add their comments. But remember — a journal is like a photo album. If it's not being read occasionally, its value to your family is lost.

If you are still unconvinced as to the benefit of journaling with your family, consider the following story.

A Reason to Remember

An old wooden trunk sits in a dusty corner of my shed, worn leather straps buckled loosely across its lid. Among the items inside is a pile of faded diaries, their tarnished keys dangling from frayed ribbons. The pages are moldy and yellowed from years of storage, but the childish scrawl is still legible: "Dear Diary, Today I love Danny! I also love Kenny! Who should I love the most?" As the years pass, the handwriting matures as well as the content: "How can I know for sure Steve is the man God would have me marry?"

Keeping a diary as I grew up served no real purpose other than to talk to myself. The entries make little sense to anyone but me and sound very self-absorbed. Still, it was a habit that continued into adulthood.

Several years ago, a friend suggested I journal for a different reason: "Make your journal a memorial to God." In response to my blank look she said, "Go home and read the fourth chapter of Joshua. You'll see what I mean."

I did just that and found the chapter to be about the time when God rolled back the waters of the Jordan River for the children of Israel. What an incredible moment that must have been for the weary group of wanderers who were finally able to set foot in the

Promised Land! It seems inconceivable that they could ever forget something so extra-ordinary, yet the first thing God commanded the Israelites to do was build a memorial: "In the future, when your children ask, 'What is this monument for?' you can tell them, 'It is to remind us that the Jordan River stopped flowing when the Ark of God went across!' The monument will be a permanent reminder to the people of Israel of this amazing miracle" (Joshua 4:6–7 TLB).

Scattered throughout the Old Testament I found other incidences where God told the people to build a memorial as a reminder of how He delivered them from various circumstances. God knew that, with the passage of time, even the most vivid memories fade. Without a reminder, they are eventually forgotten.

That challenged me to change the focus of my journaling so that it could become a source of spiritual encouragement to my family in future years—proof of God's love and intervention in our lives. The results have been exciting, and now, several years later, I have three valuable reasons to continue.

It Establishes a Written Record

Each Christmas, when my family gathers at my parents' house, we enjoy reminiscing. It's surprising how differently we remember events. Our sides are soon aching from laughter as we compare our memories and try to decide whose is the most accurate.

But when I read back through my journals, I don't have to rely on my memory—the facts are there in writing. And I find dramatic answers to prayer I'd long forgotten. When I share these entries with Steve and the boys, it's like a cool drink of water on a hot day.

Landon was thirteen when he began questioning the existence of God. "Why should I pray?" he said one night. "I don't even believe in God. He never answers my prayers."

Flipping through my journal, I read Landon entries describing answers to prayer that involved him. As I read, Landon began remembering other answers. Soon our hearts were full of God, and doubts were set aside.

Another time, Tyler was struggling to understand a new math concept. I encouraged him to ask God for help.

"Oh, Mom! Prayer won't help. God doesn't care about little things like math."

Again I turned to my journal to prove otherwise. Asking him to sit down, I read one of the pages to him:

> *Tyler was very upset tonight because of a lost school book. He'll get an F tomorrow if he doesn't have it. We looked everywhere for that book—without success.*
>
> *Finally, it was time for bed. As I sat on his bed to pray with him, I suggested he ask God to help him find the book. He thought it was silly to pray about finding something we'd already looked everywhere for. Grudgingly, though, he prayed. Just as he finished his prayer, I heard him gasp. Looking up, I saw him staring at the bookshelf over his bed. There sat the missing book!*

I looked up at Tyler, who was now grinning sheepishly. "Want me to read more?" I asked.

"No, I think I'll go see if God can help me with my math."

It Builds Confidence

During a troublesome stage in Tyler's life, I was grieving my failure as a parent. I journaled my feelings and held them out to God as a prayer, pleading for His wisdom and intervention. His answer came, even as I penned my sorrow, and I wrote down the thoughts He gave me: "My hand is on Tyler. He belongs to Me. Change will come, but it will be through Me and not you, in My time and not yours." The words were an enormous comfort, and my sense of failure was assuaged.

One year later, going back through my journal, I came to that entry and laughed as I considered the changes time had brought in Tyler's life. God had kept His promise, but I would have never realized it if not for my journal because with the passage of time I had forgotten about that agonized prayer! Looking back at that record of answered prayer gives me renewed confidence for the future challenges I'll face as a parent.

Another time, I was concerned over a business decision Steve was making, convinced it was not in our best interest. For weeks I worried and argued my point. Then early one morning, as I sat with my Bible and journal, God brought to mind the image of a baseball diamond. I wrote these thoughts down quickly, knowing they were from God: "Every player is given only one position to play. If one player tries to play his position and another position, chaos reigns. You only have to be concerned with how you are playing, not how Steve is playing. Keep your eyes on Me and off the other players."

The outcome of that situation proved that God works best when I stay within my boundaries. I refer back to that entry every time a conflict comes, reminding myself that

God doesn't need my interference.

The fatter my journal grows, the surer my confidence becomes. Its pages are tangible evidence of God's Word unfolding in specific ways for my family and me.

It Instills a Sense of Heritage

The Jews were intent on passing on their history from generation to generation. Feasts were celebrated throughout the year, each one commemorating an important event in their history. As a result, their children grew up with a strong sense of heritage.

Once, on a visit to my dad's hometown, I found a box of journals my grandfather kept. He was a farmer and his brief, concise entries were mostly about his farm.

> *Rec'vd 1 1/2" rain.*
>
> *Mule is lame.*
>
> *Corn near ripe. 87° F.*

In the middle of all these lackluster notes, I found one riveting entry: "Janice Burch

Mayo born to Howard and Zella." My grandfather, whom I had never known, recorded my birth! Seeing my name written in his precise script brought unexpected tears to my eyes, and I felt proud to be a part of the Mayo heritage.

A sense of family heritage instills pride in its members. A sense of spiritual heritage instills pride in God. Both play a vital part in a healthy self-image—and journaling is a valuable tool to preserve those heritages.

I've found that writing down specific verses as I read my Bible increases my retention, so during my private devotions I began jotting down verses that emphasized the heritage we have as children of God. I didn't know how important those verses were soon to become to Landon.

His friend Luke died suddenly of an aneurysm one summer evening. Landon's initial disbelief turned into a deep, constant grief that worried me. To him, heaven was an elusive concept, but death was now a terrible reality. In an effort to comfort him, I shared some of the verses I had journaled. One in particular spoke to his situation: "No mere man has ever seen, heard or even imagined what wonderful things God has ready for those who love the Lord" (1 Corinthians 2:9 TLB).

We talked about what those things might be, and together we marveled over the fact that Luke already knew what they were.

"It makes me excited to see heaven, Mom. It's neat to imagine what God is fixing for us." That afternoon, Landon wrote Luke a letter, telling him what was happening on earth and asking him about heaven. When he was finished, he brought the letter for me to read. Then we prayed and asked God to deliver the letter to Luke.

Landon was silent for a few minutes after our prayer. "Mom," he finally asked, "I know this sounds silly, but do you think we could get a helium balloon and tie Luke's letter to it? I know it's not really going to reach heaven, but still . . ." He paused, searching for words.

"I think it's a wonderful idea," I assured him, and grabbing our coats we hurried out to the car. We stopped at a florist's shop, where Landon picked out a hot pink helium balloon, and then we drove to the top of a butte that sits in the center of our town.

We were the only ones on the butte that afternoon, and, after Landon secured the letter to the balloon, we got out of the car and he let go of the string. The sky was a blanket of clouds that day and a gentle breeze was blowing. The balloon immediately danced away from Landon's outstretched hand. We stood in silence and watched as the balloon soared higher and higher into the heavens.

"I wish God would give us a sign that He got the letter." Landon's words were so soft I almost missed them.

"Landon, God will see to it that Luke gets your letter."

"I know, but I just wish He'd give us a sign."

Side by side we stood there, watching the balloon grow smaller and smaller. Then, just before it left our range of vision, a perfect circle opened in the clouds and the balloon sailed right through!

We stood there transfixed.

"Mom!" Landon's whisper was filled with awe. *"Did you see that? God got my letter!"*

As I recorded the events of that afternoon in my journal, I knew Landon's heavenly heritage no longer seemed quite so elusive. And I also knew this would be a page we'd come back to again and again when we needed a reminder of God's love.

As I journal, I also think ahead to a nephew, nieces, or grandchildren who perhaps will have no interest in God or a desire to read the Bible. Remembering the effect that one brief entry in my grandfather's journal had on me, it's possible my journal could have an even greater effect on them. Perhaps a personal journal kept by someone who loved them will be the catalyst that brings them to God.

Making it Happen

Often, the most difficult part of journaling is finding the time. I don't journal every day or even every week, but I always keep a notebook in my purse for unexpected free time, such as waiting for my son's baseball practice to end or for a doctor's appointment.

My favorite journaling time is during my private devotions. When a particular Bible verse speaks to me, I personalize it on paper. For example, I recorded Isaiah 44:3–5 (NASB) in this way:

> *I will pour out My Spirit on your offspring*
> *And My blessing on your descendants;*
> *And they will spring up among the grass*
> *Like poplars by streams of water.*
> *Tyler will say, "I am the Lord's" . . .*
> *and Landon will write on his hand,*
> *"Belonging to the Lord."*

I write out concerns in the form of prayers and ask God to guide my thoughts as I seek solutions. Then in the following days, I record my thoughts as well as pertinent input from other sources and verses God brings to my attention. And, of course, I always record the answers.

When I changed the focus of my journaling, it was for the purpose of leaving a written record of God's work in my family. I now see it as a valuable tool in my own spiritual growth as well.

There was a time when I struggled to stay focused on my devotions. My mind kept chasing after random thoughts. Journaling provides a focus, allowing me a deeper communion with God. My journaled prayers are far more candid, my praises more intense.

Just as the Israelites continually forgot God's obvious manifestations of love, I also forgot—until I began building a memorial through my journaling. Now those pages are a constant remainder that God, who rolled back the waters of the Jordan for my ancestors, is doing just as awesome things for me and my family.

Christmas—Perfect for Preserving Memories

☒ **Key chain tree ornaments.** We buy a colorful enamel key chain from places we visit on vacation and use them as tree ornaments. Each key chain reminds us of a fun family memory as we hang them on the branches.

☒ **Scrapbook ornaments.** These are my favorites! Throughout the year, when the kids received an award or certificate, I had a color copy of it shrunk down to wallet size and laminated. Then I'd punch a hole in the top, string a bright ribbon through it, add a bow—and *voilà!* A meaningful ornament! I did the same with their homecoming and prom photos but learned to make a color copy of them first, because laminating an actual photo can damage it.

If you use this idea, be sure to include certificates and awards you and your spouse receive during the year. Kids like sharing the limelight with their parents. Also, to get more for your money, make your ornaments double sided.

☒ **Family history tree skirt.** Our tree skirt has thirty fabric ornaments ironed onto a large circle of fabric. Each Christmas we decide what the highlight of the year has been and record the event (and the year) onto one of the ornaments. When the tree skirt is full, we'll have a thirty-year record of family highlights.

TREE SKIRT DIRECTIONS

If you're not fond of sewing, purchase a plain, ready-made tree skirt and follow the instructions for adding the iron-on shapes. Otherwise . . .

Fold one 45" square piece of fabric in half lengthwise and then crosswise to form a smaller square. Fold the fabric into a triangle. Holding your finger on the point of fabric where the folds meet, fold one more time in the same direction to form a narrower triangle. From the top of the folded edge of the triangle, measure 22 ½" down the side of the fold and mark with a pen. Keeping the end of your yardstick 22½" from the top point of fabric, move the bottom of the stick 2" from the folded edge and make another mark. Continue moving the stick and marking every 2" along the lower edge of the fabric. Cut along the marking.

Back at the top point of the fabric, measure 2" down and cut along that line. Now you should have a circle of fabric with a hole in the center. Cut a straight line from the center hole to the lower edge of the fabric. This opening enables you to wrap the skirt around the tree. Finish the edges with seam tape or a serger.

Next, cut shapes (circles, squares, stars, etc.) out of a complementary solid-colored fabric. Choose a color you can write on and shapes that will give you room to write. I cut my fabric into thirty 4" circles and glued ribbons at the top to make them look like ornaments.

Using fusible fabric, iron the shapes onto the skirt. It is best to iron on all the shapes at once, rather than adding one each year. This will ensure, first, that your fabric matches and, second, that your tree skirt gets finished!

Then, each December, when decorating your tree, discuss with your family what the year's most significant event was and record it onto a shape.

Deciding what to write each year can be an interesting challenge. Some years there have been several significant occurrences in our family, making it difficult to choose which one to record. Other years it seems as if nothing noteworthy has occurred, and we really have to think to come up with something.

Adding the "Un" to Usual

The Tooth Fairy

I once asked our sons what their favorite memory was of growing up. Without hesitation they both replied, "The tooth fairy!" The tooth fairy came to our house whether anyone lost a tooth or not. Sometimes she'd leave something frivolous under their pillows, such as a piece of candy or a coin, but usually she brought more practical items: a new toothbrush, school supplies, or new underwear.

We never knew when to expect the tooth fairy, and she didn't visit all that often, but the boys always began their day with a quick peek under their pillows.

Tyler and Landon have been gone from home for some time now, but I've noticed that they've never outgrown the urge to peek under their pillows when home for a visit. I also notice that the tooth fairy hasn't outgrown her urge to leave surprises under their pillows.

Dispensing Essentials with Flair

Don't just toss your kids a new toothbrush or other needed supplies when you can make a small event of the presentation. For instance:

- Gift wrap the item and use it as a favor when you set the table.

- Leave it on their pillow with a love note.

- Hide it in their backpack or some other place they're least likely to expect it.

More Ways to Add "Un" to Usual

☒ **Surprise notes.** I doubt anyone tires of hearing that someone finds them special. Hiding notes in lunches, drawers, backpacks, glove compartments, shoes—any place you can think of—will never fail to bring a smile to the recipient and lighten the load he might be carrying that day.

My mother wrote a silly little poem on the napkin she put in my school lunch every day. I'm talking very silly! One day she wrote:

> *I love you little, I love you big,*
>
> *I love you like a little pig!*

As corny as they were, I loved those notes and saved every napkin for years. My friends also enjoyed them and waited eagerly for me to read the poem aloud each day at lunch. My best friend tried to get her mom to write poems on her napkins, but the poor woman's expertise did not lie in poetry. She finally gave up when Lana told her that everyone laughed at her attempts to rhyme.

☒ **An occasional "breakfast in bed."** What usually defeats good intentions is when our efforts become too elaborate. Keep it simple. By breakfast in bed I mean a bowl of cereal or even a toaster pastry. No extra work for you, just something different for them.

☒ **Sunday Suitcase.** I met a man who, one Sunday a month, put something in an old suitcase. After church, he'd hand it to his kids, and whatever they found inside was their afternoon activity. A pair of car keys meant they were going for an afternoon drive—wherever the kids wanted to go. Sometimes they found a game, or swimming tickets, or a video along with a coupon for pizza.

☒ **Family Fun Night.** This is exclusive entertainment for your family alone—no friends allowed. Watch videos, play games, do whatever your family enjoys, but limit the activity to immediate family only. It's easy to let your kids' friends tag along on family outings, and sometimes that's great, but families also need to be alone with each other. It's the best way to build family camaraderie.

Miscellaneous Tips

Live "Close"

One piece of advice I received when Tyler and Landon were toddlers proved to be very valuable. It came from my cousin Neree, a mother of four, for whom parenting is a natural skill. "If you want your family to be close," she said, "live close."

Our home has three bedrooms, and when Landon was born we set his crib up in the spare room. After Neree's advice, however, I moved him into Tyler's room, and for the next fifteen years the boys shared their space. Although Tyler and Landon are very different, they learned to cohabitate quite pleasantly and indeed grew up very close.

At the beginning of Tyler's junior year, we decided he should have his own room to prepare him for his eventual departure from our home. The boys were excited about the prospect and happily separated into their own domains—until bedtime. Then, every night for nearly a year, they navigated to the same room to sleep.

This is the idea I imagine you're most likely to reject outright, thinking you'd have one endless fight on your hands if you suddenly made siblings share living space. Depending on the ages of your kids, you're probably right. But if your kids are still quite young (and of course, the same sex), consider a shared room.

With houses getting bigger and bigger, and everyone tucked away in rooms of their own, it's easy for kids and even spouses to feel independent from the rest of the family unit. This feeling is exacerbated when family members have their own televisions, video games, or computers in their rooms. The independence can easily turn into isolation.

The fact is, the more a family is called on to share, the more dependent they become on getting along well together. Learning to be compatible with family members is the first step in learning compatibility with others.

Consider limiting the number of televisions in your house to one. This will provide abundant opportunity for your kids to learn negotiation skills as well as how to give in gracefully when outvoted. The added advantage is that you're always together when watching television!

On Turning Eighteen

For Tyler's eighteenth birthday I mailed letters to friends, relatives, teachers, our pastor, his youth director, our mechanic—anyone I could think of.

"Please send your favorite piece of advice, most valuable lesson ever learned, favorite saying or Bible verse," I requested, explaining that I wanted to put together an album of advice for Tyler as he headed into adulthood. I even mailed letters to the president, our governor and senators, mayor, and chief of police. To my delight, most everyone responded!

As the letters poured in, I switched from the album idea, which would have been very simple, to something a bit more elaborate. (My eternal downfall—complicating the simple.) I decided to compile the responses into a book entitled *Lessons Already Learned—Collected Bits of Wisdom.*

I entered all the responses into my computer, enhancing the pages with borders and clip art. Then I designed a cover that I had laminated and took everything down to the print shop to collate and bind. It cost less than five dollars and became an immediate treasured keepsake.

Tyler received advice of every kind, ranging from

Read the Bible every day! The REAL Bible. The King James Version. to:
Remember: Marriage and jail are two institutions easy to get into and hard to get out of.

Tyler was especially impressed to read his letters from the president and other political officials—and so was I!

The project was such a success that when Landon turned eighteen I sent out a similar letter. While the president and other non-family members were again quick to respond, our relatives weren't so enthusiastic the second time. Their responses weren't nearly as inspired, and most never got around to sending any. Family! What can I say? It's just a good thing we only had two kids, or the third child would have received no advice at all on his eighteenth birthday!

Not wanting Landon's book to be thinner than Tyler's, I sent letters to his friends as well. (For Tyler I'd only solicited advice from adults.) To my surprise, some of Landon's most clever and inspirational advice came from his friends.

The one problem with these two gifts is that I liked them so much I hated to give them up! I wish I'd made two copies—one for them and one for me!

The Most Important Tip of All

Cherish the Season

I remember the day God demonstrated the magnitude of His love for me. It was a bleak day, many years ago when, awash with self-pity, I'd lost complete sight of who or even why I was. Thoroughly quagmired in the "terrible twos" of parenting—a stage that began early and lingered long at our house—I could see no light at the end of the tunnel.

The day began with the usual early morning activities, but I was trying to rush everyone through them. Company was coming, and I wanted to clean house. I had finished the living room and begun cleaning the family room when I heard whispered giggles coming from my two sons. With a sense of foreboding, I tiptoed to the doorway and gasped in dismay at the sight before me.

"Doesn't the living room look pretty, Mommy?" Four-year-old Tyler held a giant-sized empty jar of silver glitter while two-year-old Landon danced around in happy circles. The entire room—carpet, couch, coffee table, everything—glittered like a giant Fourth of July sparkler!

Banishing the boys to their room to play with Legos, I dragged the vacuum back into the living room and started over. By the time the living room was restored to its original shape, my schedule was in shambles and I was exhausted.

Stepping up my pace, I returned to the family room. "Look, Mommy! We're helping," smiled the boys in delight. This time the empty container was an economy-size can of Comet cleanser. I was too shocked to even gasp as I surveyed the scene before me. The floor, each piece of furniture, and every book, plant, and knickknack were covered with a fine layer of the bluish-white grit.

But the worst was yet to come. The last room to be cleaned was the master bedroom that we'd recently carpeted in a luscious shade of pale pink. As I walked into the room, my attention was immediately drawn to a large, black spot smack in the middle of the floor. Beside it sat an empty bottle of permanent black ink. I crumpled to my knees in tears.

That's pretty much how our days went during those preschool years. We bounced from disaster to disaster: perfume poured out on my new satin bedspread, the phone cord cut with scissors while I was talking on the phone. If it could be poured, dumped, sprinkled, or sprayed, Tyler and Landon did it. There was no shelf the two of them couldn't find a way to reach, no lid they couldn't get off.

A phone call to my mom after I discovered the ink did not bring the expected sympathy. "Honey," she replied, "I know it feels like this time will never end, but believe me, a blink of your eye and it'll be gone. You have to find a way to cherish this season of your life."

It was not what I wanted to hear! But I knew she was right. I just didn't know how to switch from a surviving to a cherishing mode. I began to pray every morning, asking God to help me enjoy just that one day. God's response was to make me aware of some habits I'd fallen into that squashed my capacity for joy. As I worked to change those habits, life in the Mathers' home began to lighten up.

HABIT #1: *I Overused the Word* No

Some days it seemed I'd forgotten how to say "yes." One afternoon I jotted down everything I said "no" to on a regular basis. Looking over the completed list, I discovered that, while some items involved my sons' safety and behavior, far too many were because their requests were simply inconvenient. It would make a mess or take too much time.

The boys loved to pull their chairs up to the kitchen sink and play in the water while I did dishes, but this slowed me down and made a watery mess. And I almost always refused to let them play with a huge jug that held our spare change—for no better reason than the time it took to put the coins back in the jar. Now, I decided to remove these two activities from my "no" list.

The next morning, to the boys' delight, I filled the sink with warm water and told them to bring their chairs and have at it. This simple activity kept them so well entertained, I finished my morning chores in record time. Later, when I sat down to do the bookkeeping for our business, I lugged the jug of coins over to my desk and gave Tyler and Landon permission to play with them.

Removing just those two "noes" made a tremendous difference. The boys thought I was wonderful, and I was pretty impressed with them. As a bonus, my kitchen was cleaner than ever, thanks to all the splashed water, and my bookkeeping more accurate without their usual interruptions.

HABIT #2: *The Comparison Trap*

One afternoon, waiting in line to pick up the boys from school, I noticed a bumper sticker on the car in front of mine. "My child is an Honor Student at Pilot Butte," it boasted. Glancing around I saw another with a similar sticker. And then another. Suddenly, it seemed my car was the only one lacking such a badge of success. Overcome with guilt I whimpered, "If I was a better mother, I'd have a bumper sticker too."

Another time, Landon came home from school, distraught because he'd been the only one of his friends cut from the baseball team. I tried to comfort him, but at the same time longed for someone to comfort me, again feeling I had somehow let him down.

As a parent, the comparison trap was very easy to fall into. I measured my success as a parent by the faulty yardstick of the progress and behavior of my friends' children—and invariably came up short. I forgot about God's incredible creation process. The Bible tells us that He has a unique plan for every human being. One child may walk at eight months, another at two years. One may get straight A's effortlessly, another struggles to maintain C's. It doesn't mean one child is better or their parents more adept—it's just proof of their God-given uniqueness. God gives everyone exactly the abilities needed for His plan for their life.

HABIT #3: *Not Enough Laughter*

Proverbs 15:15 (NKJV) promises, "A merry heart has a continual feast," but during my sons' preschool years I was becoming emotionally anorexic. I forgot that there is something humorous to be found in almost every situation. Still, I wanted the sound of my laughter to be familiar to my sons, so I began asking God to help me find the humor in our days. It wasn't an easy task.

After one particularly trying day with my preschoolers, I escaped to a long, steamy shower, leaving Steve to oversee the boys. I had just gotten dressed when our neighbor dropped by for coffee. As she followed me to the kitchen, she stopped abruptly.

"Interesting . . ." she murmured, studying the dining room floor. "We've always kept our catsup in the refrigerator."

I followed her gaze to a giant, red puddle circled neatly on the carpet. Steve and the boys were nowhere to be seen. Instantly, embarrassment and anger inflated my chest. Then I caught the "Hey, lighten up!" twinkle in my neighbor's eye, and we both burst into laughter. There's something about laughter that helps shrink things down to manageable proportions.

All too soon I learned that my mother was right. The preschool years indeed passed in the blink of an eye. But it wasn't just those years that vanished in a moment—it was all of childhood. One moment we were reading Mother Goose and the next moment it was college catalogs. In the process I learned that those same three habits, left unchecked, had the potential to suck the pleasure from all stages of parenting.

As Tyler and Landon grew older, I discovered that an overuse of "no" made them feel untrustworthy. The first time Landon asked to go camping with friends, I refused to even consider it. He angrily accused me of not trusting him. Although he was wrong, I couldn't really explain the fear that made me say "no."

When Steve suggested my refusal might be based in a reluctance to let Landon grow up, I knew he was right. We all sat down together, then, and laid out clear plans for the camp-out. Landon had a great time, and I survived, thanks to several calls he made to reassure me he was OK.

Several weeks later, when he asked to go to an unsupervised party, I again said "no." This time he was disappointed, but not angry. He knew I trusted him—just not the circumstances.

My temptation to compare raged strongest when it was time for my sons to pursue plans beyond high school. Listening to other parents talk about the colleges their kids were applying to and hearing of the scholarships they were receiving, my insecurities burst into full bloom. I heard myself sound apologetic about Tyler's plans to work before going to school. Not until I caught the same sound of apology in Tyler's voice did I realize I was passing my insecurities on to Tyler. That was the last thing I wanted to bequeath my son. Asking God's forgiveness, I determined to focus squarely on God—not on other people. Every morning I ask God to help me do just that.

And finally, a healthy dose of humor has been invaluable in every stage of parenting. Learning and teaching our boys to find the humor in difficult or embarrassing situations has always served to defuse the tension.

One day, Landon stormed through the house looking for a twenty-dollar bill he'd lost. He fussed and fumed, just barely suppressing the urge to accuse the rest of us of stealing it. Everyone was getting rather testy when Landon suddenly stopped in mid-rage and burst out laughing.

"I just remembered where my money is," he announced. "I hid it from myself so I wouldn't spend it."

Instantly the tense atmosphere lifted, and we all joined him in laughter. No doubt about it, laughter works magic.

Most important of all, as my sons matured, I found that the everyday traumas that accompany each stage of parenting come with valuable life lessons tucked inside. That was made clear the day I found the ink on my carpet. I called every cleaner in town for advice on removing the stain. The only solution, they said, was to cover it with a rug.

I just couldn't accept that. I had to try something.

Getting a basin of water and a washcloth, I began soaking up the ink and rinsing out the cloth. Soaking . . . rinsing . . . soaking . . . rinsing . . . Tears mingled with prayers as I worked, and soon chubby little hands were patting me on the back.

"We're sorry, Mommy," they said, and while Tyler ran to get more water, Landon brought a bar of soap. Together we worked, and gradually, before our disbelieving eyes, the spot that should have been permanent, permanently disappeared.

That was the day I discovered that God looks on mothers with a very special kind of love. Raising children is a sacred responsibility He has given to us. He knows our insecurities, our frustrations, our desire to be worthy of His trust. And sometimes, just when we need it most, He goes out of His way to prove His love. Tucked away with my cleaning supplies is a reminder of this. It is the cloth I used to clean the carpet. To this day it remains stained with permanent black ink!

Every morning for fourteen years I woke my sons up with steaming cups of hot cocoa. I can't begin to guess how much money I spent on the stuff during that time, but I do know we had some great moments of communication while sipping hot cocoa and discussing our plans for the day.

I remember very clearly, though, the first morning there was no one to wake up with a cup of hot cocoa. The day before, our youngest son, Landon, had loaded up his car and headed for school in California. I kept my composure through our good-byes, but as I watched him back out of the driveway, a rush of panic grabbed me. I couldn't let him go!

Without thinking, I jumped into my car and followed him down the driveway and all the way through town, staying far enough behind that he couldn't see me but close enough that I could see him. Only when he passed by the city limits sign did I pull off the road and watch his car disappear down the highway. Then I dropped my head to the steering wheel and cried. I cried as if my life was ending, the tears flooding down my face, dropping off the steering wheel and into my lap, where a circle of dampness grew steadily larger.

Eventually there were no tears left, and I sat there feeling emptier than an old, abandoned farmhouse. Finally, exhausted, bereft, I turned my car around and drove home.

The next morning, curled up in my favorite "quiet time" chair with a fresh cup of hot coffee, I opened my Bible and sat quietly with the Lord, contemplating the various seasons of a parent's life. I thought of the day, all those years ago, when a simple can of hot cocoa had transformed what had been a very dark season into one of challenge and pleasure. Since that day, cocoa has been a tangible "memorial" to God for me. The sight of it, the taste of it, the feel of the warm cup in my hand, reminds me of the day God rolled back the black waters of a rushing river in my life and set my feet on dry, stable ground.

As I thought about that first can of hot cocoa and all the others that followed it, I wondered just how much money I *had* spent on it over the years. Slowly, the glimmer of a new idea began to appear. *Why, with all the money I'd be saving on cocoa, just imagine the fun I could plan for my husband and me in this new season of life!*

Gulping down my coffee, I hurried in to wake Steve. A new day had dawned and it promised to be a good one!

Since 1894, Moody Publishers has been dedicated to equip and motivate people to advance the cause of Christ by publishing evangelical Christian literature and other media for all ages, around the world. Because we are a ministry of the Moody Bible Institute of Chicago, a portion of the proceeds from the sale of this book go to train the next generation of Christian leaders.

If we may serve you in any way in your spiritual journey toward understanding Christ and the Christian life, please contact us at www.moodypublishers.com.

> *"All Scripture is God-breathed and is useful*
> *for teaching, rebuking, correcting and training*
> *in righteousness, so that the man of God may be*
> *thoroughly equipped for every good work."*
> —2 TIMOTHY 3:16, 17

MOODY
PUBLISHERS

THE NAME YOU CAN TRUST

FINDING ADVENTURE IN THE ORDINARY TEAM

ACQUIRING EDITOR:
Elsa Mazon

COPY EDITOR:
Anne Scherich

BACK COVER COPY:
Julie Allyson-Ieron, Joy Media

COVER DESIGN:
Ragont Design

INTERIOR DESIGN:
Ragont Design

PRINTING AND BINDING:
Versa Press Incorporated

The typeface for the text of this book is
AGaramond